Also By Carlos Pappalardo:

Nostalgias y Otros Sentimientos

Mi Insomnio, Tu Sueño

Humanism and Verse

Páginas Sueltas

Poesía y Pacifismo

Ahimsa (Against Violence)

By Carlos Pappalardo

Copyright © 2005 by Carlos Pappalardo
All rights reserved. No part of this publication may be reproduced or transmitted by any means, electronic, mechanical, or otherwise, including photocopying and recording, or by any information storage or retrieval system, without permission – in writing – from the publishers.

Library of Congress Catalogue Number

Carlos Pappalardo
Ahimsa (Against Violence)

Edition by:

Global Publishing Sales, LLC
www.GlobalPublishingSales.com

6590 Scanlan Avenue
Saint Louis, MO 63139

ISBN 10: 1-933635-05-3
ISBN 13: 978-1-933635-04-0

To my grandchildren, Cecilia, Hugo, Charlie and Nate.
May you live in a world of peace.

"The road to the future is always under construction"
~ Anonymous

ABOUT THE AUTHOR

Carlos Pappalardo is a physician born in Argentina. He has resided in the United States since 1954. In 1992 he published his first book of poems in Spanish, NOSTALGIA Y OTROS SENTIMIENTOS, in 1996, MI INSOMNIO, TU SUEÑO, in Spanish and English, in 2001, HUMANISM AND VERSE, in English and PAGINAS SUELTAS in Spanish, in 2005 POESIA Y PACIFISMO in Spanish.

Introduction

Carlos Pappalardo has once again given us beautiful examples of his ideas and his sentiments in these well crafted and eloquent poems. As is his custom, they range from the bitter to the sweet. The first section, on" Non-Violence," expresses in powerful and evocative phrases his own horror at the stupidity and waste of war, especially as it affects the youngest and most innocent.

Using his pen as effectively in his avocation as he wielded his scalpel in his vocation, he underscores the hypocrisy of political and religious leaders as they wave the flags of patriotism or flaunt the pages of holy books to lead the unthinking into the unthinkable. What a noble hope that we could make love, in the broadest sense-love for humanity-and not war and find moderation in the midst of extremism.

Supporters of President George W.Bush will not find much comfort in these pages. But Carlos is an equal-opportunity critic. He has little patient for either dubiously-elected politicians who wield patriotic slogans to justify the most heinous acts or self-selected messiahs who use terrorism as an indiscriminate tool to achieve domination.. And more fundamental for him than what a particular leader may say or do is what lies at the bottom of the human heart, a heart that these days is too often led astray by manipulated passions rather than the better angels of our spirit. "Why Don't You Cry Soldier?,"he asks rhetorically, when confronted with the terrible damage and destruction of his or her actions. "How Many More"must die before kindness and generosity can prevail?

How to restore the individual choice, reason, and humanity that should connect us all is one of his mayor preoccupations, especially in this increasingly technological and impersonal world. And in this as in many other ways, he leads by example, crafting poems that express his own individuality and outrage in a way that he share with the rest of us, using the very technology that can both liberate and slave us.

While the first section may be the "bitter," the second section, "Miscellaneous," is definitely the "sweet." In a series of exquisitely-rendered word portraits, Carlos mediates on the beauties and wonders of nature, the joys and frustrations of aging, and the rewards and satisfactions of children and grandchildren. Particularly evocative are his meditations on his own offspring as well as in"Scar od Innocence" his great feelings for the many"little angels"whose lives he has enhanced through his skills as a surgeon. In this, as in so many of his poems, his warmth, kindness, and generosity shines through.

Whatever anger Carlos has with the current state of affairs, when some humans seem bent on destroying others as well as the earth we all inhabit, signs of humanity and optimism persist and prevail in his work. His legacy for us and for his children will be measured not only in personal accomplishments and material rewards, but also in the many provocative and powerful thoughts he provides through his words of insight and inspiration, words that call upon us to consider our own humanity and place in the universe and to leave the world better than we found it. What nobler interprise could there be?

Richard Walter
(Professor of History at Washington University, St. Louis, Missouri)

Preface

For most of my adult life I have been an ardent admirer of Mahatma Gandhi's position against violence. While I was reading one of his books I ran into the word AHIMSA, which he translates as non violence. Talking about this with my son Rickie he suggested the word as title for my book.

These poems are not written merely to proyect a political view but rather as a cry for peace and understanding. My words of gratitude to Richard Walter for his expressive and kind introduction and to Bruno Cinellu, who designed such expressive cover.

Carlos Pappalardo

Part of the proceeds of this book will be donated to Doctors Without Borders.

TABLE OF CONTENTS

CHAPTER 1: NON-VIOLENCE 1

Pacifist 3

Moderation 5

Borrowed Space, Violent Times 7

A Plea Against Violence 9

Peace 11

Manual Expressions 13

It Doesn't Matter 15

Wings of Madness 17

Patriotism 19

Voices from Iraq 21

In Defense of Peace 23

Why Don't You Cry Soldier? 25

Dream at the Dawn of the 21st Century 27

Mars (You God of War) 29

Conflict of Voices 31

Tears 33

How Many More? 35

Osama 37

Before Departure 39

Why? 41

Praise the Lord 43

Post Election Blues (2004) 45

CHAPTER 2: MISCELLANEOUS 47

Electronic Friendship 49

Monday's Review 51

Wake Me Up in April 53

New Year's Eve 55

Standing Female Nude 57

And Then..59

Spider Web 61

Indifference...63

My Three Children 65

Life as a Journey..67

My Granddaughter's Seventh Birthday..............69

In Motion 71

Lunar Stillness...73

Seasons 75

Unauthorized Biography of Myself....................77

After Sunset 79

From Aspen To Denver 81

Molecular Journey.....................................83

Scar of Innocence......................................85

Inquiring 87

When Tomorrow Comes..........................89

Non-Violence

Non-violence is not a garment to be put on and off at will. Its seat is in the heart, and it must be an inseparable part of our very being.

~ Mahatma Gandhi

PACIFIST

Some of my friends
quite anxious to put a label
on everyone
have called me "pacifist"
Is it, perhaps, because
I have the habit
of seeing hunger and war
as the most despicable affront
man can inflict?
or maybe, because
when they asked me
to choose between two reds,
I've always rejected
the red of blood
for the other more inviting
of lipstick?

MODERATION

And the media with its glamorous
display of novelties, gives us:

Liberals and conservatives,
left wingers and right wingers,
progressives and regressives,
doves and hardliners,
warmongers and pacifists,
tree huggers and petrol lovers
humanists and consumerists,
the socially conscious and tax conscious,
activists and reactionaries…

And the list goes on and on
and the thoughts leap into words,
of empty rethoric or insults.
Logic is bypassed by a bridge
which runs from the shores
of the "right" extreme
to the shores of the"wrong" extreme.

Can anybody tell me
where is "Mister in-between?"

BORROWED SPACE, VIOLENT TIMES

In those moments when
I'm trying to forget
the uncertain path
of my inadequacies
I allow my soul
to take refuge
among the mysteries
of the world
of solitude and silence.
Not to blur what sorrounds me
nor to curse what my mind
can not touch nor bend,
rather, to admire with reverence
the immensity and beauty
of this, our Universe.
Then,
    I emerge from the depth
of my self imposed exile
asking always the same question…
"why must creatures of this world
engender such violence
when they are but leasing
their teluric space
for only just a while?

BORROWED SAGE,
VIOLENT TIMES

In those moments when
I'm trying to forget
the uncertain parts
of my inadequacies

I allow my soul
to take refuge
among the mysteries
of this world
of solitude and silence.

Not to hate what surrounds me,
nor to envy what my mind
can not touch nor bend,
rather, to admire such treasures
the immensity and beauty
of this, our Universe.
Then,
I emerge from the depths
of my self imposed exile
asking always the same question...
why must creatures of this world
engender such violence
when they are here having
this robust spirit
for only just a while?

A PLEA AGAINST VIOLENCE

From high on their pulpit of faith
we hear the voices
of wise, righteous men:
"God created life
and only God can take it away".

From high on their pulpit of faith
they admonish us
about our serious misdeeds
because the justice
of our fellow "man-God"
may fall upon us
as a sentence of death.

From high on their pulpit of faith
they quote verbatim
from that book of gospels
which exhorts us
to turn the other cheek,
but, in the following page
it says "an eye for an eye".
Which one shall we follow?
if we chose the latter
"the whole world will be blind".

Ah…if they would just descend
from their pulpit of faith
perhaps, they'll perceive
the tragic extent
of violence on Earth.

A PLEA AGAINST VIOLENCE

From high on their pulpit of faith
 we hear the voices
of some, righteous men
 "God created life
and only God can take it away".

From high on their pulpit of faith
 some admonish us
about our serious mistake
 to oppose the justice
of our fellow "man–God"
 who kill upon us
as a sentence of death.

From high on their pulpit of faith
 they quote us verses
From that book of yesyes
 which advises us
to turn the other cheek,
 but, in the following page
it says "an eye for an eye",
Which one shall we follow?
 if we chose the latter
the whole world will be blind.

And... if they would just descend
 from their pulpit of faith,
 perhaps, they'll perceive
 the tragic scenes
 of violence on Earth.

PEACE

Someone, once said:
"loneliness is the emptiness
of being alone,
solitude is the fullness
of being alone".

Now that I've finished
my dialogue with the healed
wounds of loneliness,
I look,
almost with contentment,
for moments of serenity
embracing , unabashedly,
those slumberous hours
of these, my wiser days.

I dive below the surface
of the night, deeper and deeper,
not to blur reality
along the way
or to search for ecstacy or bliss
but, hopefully, to find
that elusive lady,
unseen for many years
on our planet and who
we know as PEACE>

MANUAL EXPRESSIONS

Did you ever wonder
about the expressive
language of hands
which tells us so much
with their silent voices?

The sad hands of "good-byes."
The tender hands of a mother,
palm- to- palm in prayers
or caressing a child.
The sincere ones
with the firm grip
of the loyal friend.
The sensuous touch of lovers.
The trembling hands
of fear or pain.
The deformed, spotted hands
of the elderly, slowed down
by the burden of years.
The harmonious hands
that sprinkle sounds
from a cello or a harp.
The harsh fist of cruelty
of the inquisitor.

Now that the aseptic,
electronic age is here,
what would the anonymous hands
of the innocent soldier say
when he or she must kill
without knowing who or how
only by pressing a key?

IT DOESN'T MATTER

*It would almost seem
that nobody cares
who drops the bombs,
may they be nuclear,
precision, smart, napalm
or selective ones.
It doesn't matter
where or when....*

*It seems it doesn't matter
where they fall,
far away Hiroshima,
Nagasaki, Korea,
Bosnia or Afghanistan.
Upon impact
crowds of "somebodies"
will be "nobodies".*

*It doesn't matter,
for the horror
is always the same:
ghostly silhouettes
of towns and forests
and torn illusions
of a thousand men.*

It doesn't matter.

IT DOESN'T MATTER

It would almost seem
that nobody cares
who drops the bombs,
may they be nuclear,
precision, smart, napalm
or cluster ones.
It doesn't matter
when or where.

Be seven it about what's
where they fall,
far away Hiroshima,
Nagasaki, Korea,
Bosnia or Afghanistan.
Upon impact
enough of "somebodies"
will be "nobodies".

It doesn't matter
for the terror
is always the same,
ghost, silhouettes
of torn out forms
and torn lifetimes
of a thousand suns.

It doesn't matter

15

WINGS OF MADNESS

*The wings of madness
have spread across the Atlantic
casting wide shadows
over the land of oil and sand.*

*Lurking in the darkness,
self-appointed
"sons of Allah"
answer with legislated violence
with terror and fear
and among the innocents
smiles fade in quivering lips.*

*Prayers fail to be enough,
hope is anemic and terse.
Are we running out of tears?
Are we running out of excuses?
Maybe so,
but sadly for Humanity
we're not running out
of that black, subterranean curse.*

Nov. 19 004

PATRIOTISM

*"The naïve patriotism is limited
to a geographic horizon"*
(José Ingenieros)

*From infancy
they injected in the strata
of your innocent mind
the rigid concept
of a "blessed" land.*

*They taught you
how to wrap yourself
in your "glorious" flag
and how to describe
with debasing words
(fanatics, evildoers)
those unknown to you
who carry the blemish
of being born in a foreign soil.*

*Through the years
you were blinded by the narrow,
selfish vision of your borders.
It's time to walk away
from your "moralizing" geography
to learn that those in other lands
breathe, play, love, cry
and sing like you.
They see the same moon,
their sun is the same.*

They also have a history, perhaps,
much richer than yours
and just like you , they know as much
of scorn and injustice,
falsehood or truth.

With our time and space
so limited,
you must open the windows
of your blind patriotism
to set free
the exaggerated sense
of your own importance
and let in the splendor
of a Universal embrace.

VOICES FROM IRAQ

I am that child
  who was left behind
  missing his parents
  missing one limb.

I am that woman
  who like many others
  has no children
  to hold in my arms.

I am that man
  who lost the means
  to feed his own
  now, pressed hard,
  what shall I choose…
  vengeance or hatred?

I am that teacher
  who nourished innocent minds.
  Where would we gather now
   away from sun and dust?
  My school is gone.

I am the soldier
  who, with spins and lies,
  was sent to "liberate"
  a distant land,
  not knowing,
  if perhaps I'll die.

I am the doctor
>*who treated the wounds,*
>*only those*
>*the eyes could see.*

I am the essence
>*of every living soul*
>*and even though*
>*my flesh was torn*
>*by the swords of men*
>*of misguided thoughts,*
>*they still call me:*
>**HUMANITY**

IN DEFENSE OF PEACE

*Why is it no longer an honor
to speak in defense
of peace and the truth?*

*It seems irrelevant
to dwell on pacifism
while the world burns
in the expanding flames
of hate and terrorism.
And becomes louder
the repugnant choir
of missiles and bombs.*

*The virus of violence
with the blessings
of counterfeiters of faith
keep breeding more orphans,
keep breeding more graves.*

*Meanwhile..
the "Lord of the land",
ever so pious,
ever so eager
defends his bellicose blunders
with one hand on the bible
and one on the trigger.*

C.
P. 2-17-06

WHY DON'T YOU CRY SOLDIER?

*What do you feel, Soldier,
when you fire a weapon
like the "smart" bomb
not smart enough to know
how much pain it'll cause…?*

Why don't you cry, Soldier?

*Have tears been forbidden
in your fratricidal school?*

*Have they taught you
to silence your tender mind
with absolute amnesia
of feelings or reason?*

*Have they wrapped you
in your maternal flag,
all, in order to protect
interests that are not now
nor will ever be yours?.*

*Or perhaps…
because they made you defend
ostentatious billboards
painted in dry blood,
offering with grandiloquent stench
a warlike philosophy
for greater consumption.*

Why don't you cry, Soldier?

Don't those children without shelter,
without parents, without limbs
move you in some way?.
What of that mother
who now must kiss
another's son instead?

Why don't you cry, Soldier?

Perhaps, at the edge of the night
in the front lines of your conscience
you'll engage in dialog
with your fatigue and your fears
emptying the faults
of your pre-ordered actions.
and when you think of those you love
and of promises left behind,
perhaps then, Soldier, your pillow
will be dampened with tears.

April 17 2003

DREAM AT THE DAWN OF THE 21st CENTURY

...And we welcome the new century
with that hope and that dream
reserved for the new born.

Remember?
We thought the right to dream was all ours
and we found so easy
to think of a new world
without war,
without starving children,
without faces of leaders
inebriated with power.

Did we fantasize
about questions,
about replies?
Who do we ask now,
in what tone?
Now, when more than three years
are gone by
and the dewdrops of hopes and dreams
have failed to crystallize.
Who do we ask
now that Gandhi and Socrates are gone?

Both the stage and actors
are the same:
the flag waving patriotic preachers

of misguided heroism,
the hate, the vengeance,
the thirst for blood and oil,
all remains the same,
as the ever present shadow
of sinister terrorism.

MARS (YOU GOD OF WAR)

*I have lived the days
when wonders sprang up everywhere,
when the quest for knowledge
fueled man's creativity,
not enough, however,
to quell the insatiable
appetite of Mars,
who, Minerva called:
"ferocious, senseless,
infernal God".*

*They did not listen then,
they do not listen now.
There is always someone to blame,
so, man keeps trying to extinguish.
fire with fire.
Without change of course
our fragile world
will ignite in flames*

*I have lived the days
when, with arrogant speed
science grew manifold,
not enough, however,
to create a vaccine
against hunger, violence or war.*

MARS (YOU GOD OF WAR)

I have lived the day
when wonders sprang up everywhere,
when the quest for knowledge
fueled man's creativity,
not enough, however,
to quell our insatiable
appetite of Mars,
who Minerva called
"Most un-sensible
imbecilic God."

They did not listen then,
they do not listen now.
There is always someone to blame,
or with hopes trying to extinguish
fire with fire.
Without change of course
our fragile world
will ignite in flames.

I have lived the days
when, with arrogant speed
science grew manifold,
not enough, however,
to create a universe
against hunger such as ours.

CONFLICT OF VOICES

There are days when you feel
irremediably alone.
When the whole world
seems to be suffering
from incurable loneliness
and you are the only one
who realizes it.
In those days you would like
to close your eyes
and return to the child
who with innocent ears
used to hear
the irreproachable,
comfortable voice
of parents and teachers.
That soothing sound,
almost musical,
that taught of love,
honor, duty and letters.
But that distant voice
is no longer here,
it has given way
to the voice of the moment,
the heartless sound of the media
which has kidnapped the air
and tells us ad nauseam
of crime, violence, war,
terrorism and despair.

CONFLICT OF VOICES

There are days when you feel
irremediably alone.
When the whole world
seems to be suffering
from insensible loneliness
and you are the only one
who realizes it.
In these days, you would like
to close your eyes
and return to the child
who with innocence can
used to hear
the irreproachable
confortable voice
of a mute and unknown
That soothing sound
almost mystical
that taught, at least
honor, duty and letters.
But that distant voice
is no longer here,
it has given way
to the voice of the moment,
a terrifies sound of the media
which has kidnapped the so
called child that we
were once when
silence began.

TEARS

There are more than enough tears,
I told you so,
many more than you believe,
look no further
than the weeping willow
or the crocodile,
the inconsolable widow,
the physical pain
or the spoiled child.

Without being a historical novelty,
there are new tears
that have appeared
with undesirable frequency
in a land of chaos
newly "liberated"
by a "compassionate leader"
who "can do no wrong".

They are the tears
of orphan children
(and mother in mourning)
who weep and ask:
WHY?,
FOR HOW LONG?

November 14 04

(translated from Spanish by Richard Pappalardo)

TEARS

There are more than enough tears,
I told you so,
many more than can follow
look no further
than the weeping willow
or the crocodile,
the inconsolable widow,
the physical pain
or the spoiled child.

Without being a unisexual novelty
there are even tears
that have appeared
with unbelievable frequency
in a kind of chant
"unde-blu-eared"
by a "Tompu-warsa lender"
who "can do no wrong".

They are the tears
of orphan children
(and mothers in mourning)
who weep and ask
WHY,
FOR HOW LONG?

November 14, 04

(translated from Spanish by Rithuel Pippalotolo)

HOW MANY MORE?

How many more must die,
how many more must bear
lingering clouds
of fear and despair?

How many more tears
must Humanity shed
while our new Empire
dictates terms of "peace"
at the cannon's mouth?

How many more times
must the World witness
each Imperial power
peddling "democracy"
with self deception,
manufactured ambiguity
and misrepresentation?

Aggression is camouflaged
as a "gesture of good will".
Kindness,
as a one way bridge of generosity
while resistance or self-defense
is tackled with ever more
refreshed ignorance
and willful blindness.

HOW MANY MORE

How many more must die
how many more must bear
lingering clouds
of fear and despair

How many more tears
must Humanity shed
until our own Empire
deserves array of grace
in the nations' mantle

How many more times
must the World witness
each Imperial power
peddling "democracy"
thro' self deception,
manufactured uniformity
and misrepresentation

Aggression is camouflaged
as a "gesture of good will".
Kindness
as a one way bridge of generosity
while treasures or self-defence
is tackled with ever more
sophisticated ploys or
loud unifying falsehoods

OSAMA

Last night
I saw you on the screen,
supreme commander
in the army of death,
self appointed "Lord of Islam".

I saw you with your cynical smirk
disclosing a mind filled
with insidious fantasies
lurking within the realm
of logical absurdity.

I saw you
in your messianic self absorption
gloating, describing
your diplomacy of guns,
haranguing your brave
"soldiers of Allah"
who you trained very well
for their senseless slaughter
and that of us "infidels".

I saw you,
opulent architect of destruction
sorrounded by your brood.
Fortunately, Humanity is not made
of poor-rich men like you.
So...I shall not look at your image
with contempt but pity
and whatever is left of compassion.
. 12-14-01

BEFORE DEPARTURE

When you see me sliding
into the slumberous face
of my final dream,
please, don't wake me up
unless, a catastrophic event
is shaking this unruly world.
I mean, something sensational
like a pandemic
of reason and optimism.
A massive kidnapping
of dictators and crooked politicians
(with nobody left to pay ransom).
A hurricane of hugs
and innocent kisses.
A serious heat wave
melting all the flags
and temples of hate.
A violent volcanic eruption
of symphonies and poems.
A dangerous high tide
of incurable romantics
(including the sinners)
or maybe yet
a severe thunderstorm
of peace and hope, to wash
the face of this Earth
stained with violence,
hunger and injustice.
Then…after a while,
when the disaster is over
I shall go back to my dream
with an eternal smile.

BEFORE DEPARTURE

When you are not licking
into the thunderous jaws
of my final disaster,
please, don't wake me up
unless a catastrophic event
is shaking this unruly world.
I mean, something unnatural
like a pandemic
of reason and optimism,
a sincere (right!?)
of dictators and crooked politicians
(who voluntarily to pay penance).
A banner use of hugs
and innocent kisses,
A broken bear market
melting on the flag
and troops with of hair.
A radical volcanic eruption
of guarantees and peace.
A dangerous high tide
of forceable romantics
(including the sinners)
or maybe yet
a severe thunderstorm
of peace and cups, to wash
the face of all Earth
stained with mother
anger and injustice.
Then, after a while,
when the disaster is over,
I shall go back to my dreams
with an eternal smile.

WHY?

In the news today
I heard:"yesterday
nine children were killed
in Afghanistan"
Neither hunger nor disease
were to blame,
their lives were erased
by a "smart" bomb.
The announcement was made
so "matter of fact"
after all,
they were children
from a distant land.

Without a hint of apologies
the authorities stated:
"the matter shall be
fully investigated.
It was all justified,
"ours soldiers were after
a terrorist man"
Nine more vulnerable humans
shall be now classified
as "collateral damage"
by the Pentagon

Yesterday…
nine children were killed
in Afghanistan

Dec.7 03

XLIV.

            In the news today
            I heard yesterday
            nine children were killed
              in Afghanistan.
            Neither hunger nor disease
              were to blame,
            their lives were ended
              by a "smart" bomb.
            The ominous report was made
              so "matter of fact"
              after all
              they were children
              from a distant land.

            Without a hint of apology,
              the authorities stated,
              "the matter shall be
              fully investigated.
              It was all justified,
            "our soldiers were after
              a terrorist man.
            Nine more vulnerable human
              shall be now classified
              as 'collateral damage,'
              by the Pentagon."

              Herein,
            nine children were killed
              in Afghanistan.

                    Dec 7, 03

PRAISE THE LORD

("Praise the Lord and pass the ammunition"
Words of Chaplain Howell Forgy, aboard the U.S.S.
New Orleans during a Japanese attack, December 1941)

Ah....the miracles
of this 21st century.
Who would've suspected,
it gives us a president
who was not elected
but dutifully crowned
by five supreme judges
in splendid black suits.
They told us, citizens,
to ignore that minor detail
'cause the man is a christian
and "compasionate" to boot..
We must also remember,
he came with a mission:
to destroy dictators
with weapons of death.
   "Praise the Lord
and pass the ammunition".

Ah...the wonders
of this 21st century.
It brings us the revival
of the best preachers
 money can buy.
They'll give us their messages
in the street, in the churches

*and, for a larger audience
they'll use television.
God bless Mr.Robertson,
God bless Mr.Falwell.
… "Praise the Lord
and pass the ammunition".*

*Ah…the good justice
of this 21st century,
it gives us a man
who shall put in jail
every "non-christian"
who is under suspicion.
God bless the Attorney General
"Praise the Lord
and pass the ammunition".*

POST ELECTION BLUES(2004)

(translated from Spanish by R.Pappalardo)

*Welcome to the land
where everybody enjoys
the best democracy
money can buy.
  Here, you'll find no other warlords
vying for a chance
to sign a four year lease
for that House, so big and so White.
For all it requires
is a bellicose stance
on one presidential leg
and to humbly kneel on the other
at the altar of Wall Street.
  This "compassionate" christian man
with touching humility
and direct line to heavens
tells us:
"Let us pray, for this our daily oil
 and our own security".
  So, take your seat
"O Captain, my Captain"
and let us see,
 what surprises(or horrors)
will he bring us to bear?
another pre-emptive strike?
will it be North Korea,
perhaps Syria, maybe Iran?*

*Will he keep spreading
peace and order
with his precise missiles
and his "smart" guided bombs?.*

*Who knows
what is in store for them,
who knows
what is in store for us.*

*All the while, innocent children
keep dying in Iraq
and Humanity, in dismay
burns in the pyre
of collective anger,
disbelief and despair.*

*Carlos Pappalardo
3-5-04*

Miscellaneous

A bird does not sing because he has an answer. He sings because he has a song.

~ Joan Walsh Anglund

ELECTRONIC FRIENDSHIP

No longer, dear friend,
do you come calling
at my door.
I miss the sound of your voice,
the warmth of your hands.

I know all too well…
It's not forgetfulness:
when in fact I now receive
your friendly messages
well ordered
in an electronic box

Have we lost, perhaps,
that inborn rectitude
which allows us to dialogue
with one another?

Or is it more comfortable instead
to now seek refuge
within a musty cavern
of the cybernetic world
where hours and days
are lived in series,
where the warm contact
of human beings
is filtered through a wire
and friendship,
scattered light
upon a screen.

ELECTRONIC FRIENDSHIP

No longer, dear Friend,
do you come calling
at my door
I miss the sound of your voice,
the warmth of your hands.

I know all too well.
Ill at joyer'l loses
even in fact I now receive
your friendly messages
and indeed
in an electronic box

Blase as last, perhaps
it is the new attitude
which allows us to change
with one another

Or is it more comfortable instead
to meet and rejoice
within a snugly reserve
of the cybernetic world
where hours and days
are lived in series,
where the mirror answer
of human beings
is filtered through a wire
and fira oddity,
restored light
upon a screen

MONDAY'S REVIEW

Don't sit there and dwell
about eternity
'till you've made an effort
to know your bountiful Earth.

Don't speak of freedom
after using your ballot
to elect those people
who usurp your own liberties.

Don't kneel to pray to a God
that created life
when you, patriotically claim
to bless the death penalty.

Don't try to light
candles of peace
when the only flame you have
is that of vengeance and hate.

Don't long for immortality
until you know
what to do with yourself
on a rainy Monday afternoon.

WAKE ME UP IN APRIL

Wake me up in April
  when tulips are dressed
  with opening night costumes
  and Nature paints
  with extravagant skills.

Wake me up in April
  when trees are burning
  with the anticipation
  of restless new nests
  and are proud to splurge
  on multiple shades
  of beautiful green.

Wake me up in April
  when flowers prefer
  to be seen
  rather than touched
  and even the rocks
  give birth to new life.

Wake me up in April
  when romantic souls
  find dreams in the sky,
  but I promise, instead
  I'll indulge with dreams
  made for my eyes.

WAKE ME UP IN APRIL

Wake me up in April
when tulips are dressed
with opening night costumes
and Nature paints
with consummate skill.

Wake me up in April
when trees are bursting
into the emergency
of verdant new seas
and are proud to splurge
on multiple shades
of beautiful green.

Wake me up in April
when Nature prefers
to use
nature than nurtured
and coax the rocks
gent'ly on to new life.

Wake me up in April
when cumulus souls
find dreams in the sky
but I promise, instead,
I'll indulge with dreams
while I'm my true.

NEW YEAR'S EVE

Every bubble, every bell
of every new year
reminds me
how much closer
we get to graduation
from this School of Life.

Although
I passed many subjects
with very good grades
from the time I learnt
the language of flowers
or the changes of seasons,
I must confess
I flunked just as many
when anger or haste
clouded my vision.

But, it's my intention
to take other courses
(whichever is offered)
till the time when my walk,
on the road lopsided,
will be marked
with pained hesitation.

I know very well
my diploma won't say:
"MAGNA CUM LAUDE"
but I hope, instead:
"WITH HONORS,
FOR TRYING HIS BEST".

STANDING FEMALE NUDE

*(Inspired by the bronze statue of Max Klinger
Germany, 1898 . St.Louis' Art Museum.)*

*I don't know who you are,
woman of bronze, or whether
your naked body symbolizes
 chastity or shame,
but I do feel your loneliness
when I see you there,
 on a rigid pedestal
posing still, like a beautiful butterfly
mounted in a glass case.*

*Maybe…just maybe,
your metallic, ageless flesh
conceals a speck of soul,
just a smile will tell me so.
Then, after we sneak by the curator,
 I will take you for a stroll
and in the name of beauty
I shall find you a new home
closer to Nature.
Perhaps,
you deserve a fountain,
a pristine fountain
with birds perching
on your delicate limbs,
clear drops washing
your nakedness,
silvery fishes kissing your feet*

*and the moon and the wind
caressing your face.
And maybe…just maybe,
in some distant day
I could bring to you
a man made of bronze
to share your space.*

AND THEN…..

*I was thirsty then,
when the moon came calling
at the gates of night
and my senses drove me
to a waveless lake
where I drank
the moon's reflection.*

*I was hungry then
when my senses drove me
to the orchard of pleasures
where I tasted the bitter-sweet
of still green fruits.*

*I was lonely, at times,
when my senses drove me
to flirt with death.
By chance or fortune,
she wasn't there.*

*Now that I've moved
on the eddying surface
of the stream of time
wisdom has taught me
that you don't
drink mirages,
that you wait until
the grapes are ripe
upon the vine,*

*that you don't pay court
to Lady Macabre,
let her come after
you complete your circle
and then……
turn around and die
with a thunderous,
 big, fat laughter.*

SPIDER WEB

You greeted me this morning
through the window of my eyes
as you appeared from nowhere
balancing from a silver string
or, perhaps you descended
from some magic arachnid world.
Regardless,
I watched you moving
your articulated limbs
as if they were counting atoms
from the air.
And I stood there, mesmerized
while you sculpted
your intricate trap
pulling all the geometry of Nature
into a beautiful web.

INDIFFERENCE

When you no longer have to explain
why you despise Winter
or why you feel sad, happy
or simply, ill-tempered.

When you decide to remember
  only those holidays
  and birthdays of your choice,
you'll begin to perceive, here and there,
subtle signs of indifference:
in those hands which no longer caress,
in those eyes which see you differently,
in those ears which don't hear the sound
   of your voice
     and in minds which tend to forget.
Then...
      should you decide to travel
to the Land of Memories,
searching for bits of your past,
as you go through Customs,
the Inspector of Curiosity
doesn't even bother
to open your luggage
full of counterfeit dreams.

MY THREE CHILDREN

*Many patches of time ago,
with dreams and hopes
in between,
I threw three pebbles
in that lake
where waters can be furious
or suddenly still.*

*Ever hopeful,
ever expectant,
I waited for the ripples
to reach shore.*

*And though time kidnapped
many of my years,
I rejoice to know
that they've arrived.*

*And now…I yearn
to see them grow,
to treat this Earth
as if forever
they'll live there.*

LIFE AS A JOURNEY

Before I set foot
upon that eternal
geography of obsolescence,
before that whirling, telluric sphere
evicts me from my earthly space

I shall propose to myself:

To humanize more
my humanism,
to be more suspect
of my suspicions,
to ignore the murmur
of the hidden guilt,
to criticize with louder voice
injustice and terrorism,
to flirt more with joy
and silliness,
to fight against fears
which hypnotize
logic and reason,
to protect(in my fashion)
this aging body
with all its factory flaws
as well as those I, myself
inflicted upon it.
Finally,
without any apprehension,
I shall keep moving forward
with the clear idea in mind
that life is a journey
and not a destination.

MY GRANDAUGHTER'S SEVENTH BIRTHDAY

*Do you know
my dear little Ceci
the story of seven?.
Many people and places
carry this number
from the Earth to the Heavens.*

*Seven were
the wonders of the world,
they were seven
the wise men of Greece,
a city was built
on the seven hills of Rome
and there are
seven days in a week.
We have seven liberal arts
and all the waters
of the world are referred to
as the seven seas.
Seven are the colors
of the rainbow.*

*Oops…I almost forgot
there were also
 seven deadly sins
And guess what?
on a February seven
your nonno was born.*

Now...

> *you have completed*
> *the first seven years*
> *of your sweet, innocent life.*
> *May you see many more*
> *and some day*
> *you may look back at them*
> *with a wonderful smile.*

Nonno

IN MOTION

Even when old age,
without respect,
came crashing into me
and with its wicked ways
tried to slow me down
with its array of aches and pains,
it is not my intention to sit down
and write the biography
of my woes,
nor to mourn
my long, departed youth
or my black hair.
I intend to be in motion
till the end.
I won't allow one molecule
of stillness in my body
until then.

LUNAR STILLNESS

Last night, the moon
hanging naked
from the firmament,
looked at me
like a giant, congested eye,
part concealed
by the eyelashes
of the trees

SEASONS

Regardless of how long
I've left in my journey,
regardless of what I think,
what I dream or I feel,
this old Universe
keeps saying "good morning"
every dawn.
That's why
I would like to live
the "good old days" now.

I could ask the Spring
to create more blossoms
or to keep
its crystaline brooks
in a stand-still,
I could ask the Summer
to last a bit longer.
To the colorful Autumn
to keep painting more leaves.
I could ask old man Winter
to be more gentle
with my aching frame
(at least, I could try).
But, I well know,
these orderly seasons,
oblivious of time,
have a nasty habit
of just going by.

SEASONS

Regardless of how long
I've left in my journey,
regardless of what I think,
what I dream or I feel
this old Universe
keeps saying "good morning"
every dawn.
That's why
I would like to hire
the "good old days" too.

I would ask the Spring
to create more blossoms
or to keep
its sparkling beauty
in a stand still.
I could ask the Summer
to last a bit longer.
To see colorful Autumn
to keep painting more fairer.
I could ask old man Winter
to be more gentle
with my aching frame.
So, I wish I could try.
Sure, I wish I could
hope orderly seasons
abolition of time.
have a many habit
of just going by

UNAUTHORIZED BIOGRAPHY OF MYSELF

I came to this world
on the other side of the Equator.
I was born long ago
and far-away.
(more ago than away).
They say I arrived
desperately naked
and incurably young .
From what I can remember
it felt terribly good.
But, however hard I tried
I couldn't stay that way.
I was informed there is no
"forever youth",
that the entire human race
was born to become old.
Stubbornly, in my early
years of education
I proposed to keep my pace
and following my vocation
I decided to be an actor,
but, they told me I couldn't
'cause I didn't have the face.
So, instead, I became a doctor.
And after many operations
and three kids worthy of gold
I arrived to the conclusion
that being an old foggy
is not bad after all.

UNAUTHORIZED BIOGRAPHY OF MYSELF

I came to this world
on the other side of the Equator
I was born long ago
and for many
(aeons ago that was)
They say I arrived
desperately naked
and unsmiling
From what I can remember
it felt mostly good
But somewhere/land I tried
I couldn't stay that long
I was informed there is no
"forever such"
that the entire human race
was born to become old.
Somehow, in my early
years of education
I proposed to keep my pace
and following my vocation
I decided to be a doctor,
but, they told me I couldn't
'cause I didn't have the face.
So, instead, I became a doctor.
And after many operations
and those little tooth of gold
I arrived to the conclusion
that being an old fogey
is not bad after all.

AFTER SUNSET

In his famous "Meditations"
Marcus Aurelius told us:
"the Universe is transformation,
and life is an opinion".

Now... tell me
which one is yours?,
your opinion, I mean.

Now that your face
is no longer the street
where beauty used to live
and your mind
is not crowded
with fresh fantasies.
When your body is empty
of intimacy and passion
and ceases to be
the center of gravity
for man's attractions.
Now that that you've decided
to raise the price of love
to become more desirable.

When your heart in its confusion
doesn't know what to expect,
why don't you pause
and dress yourself
with a heavy cloak of reality.?
Usually, it gets cold
after sunset.

AFTER SUNSET

In his famous "Meditations"
Marcus Aurelius told us:
"The Universe is transformation,
and life is an opinion."

                Plus... Tell me
            which one is yours,
        your opinion, I mean.

Now that your face
is no longer the street
where beauty used to live
            and your mind
            is not crowded
        with fresh fantasies
iffen your body is empty
of intimacy and passion
            and ceases to be
        the center of yours,
        for want attraction.
Now that that you be destined
to enter the prime of four,
to become more desirable.

When your desire in its emptiness
doesn't know what to expect
        why won't you pause
        and close yourself
    inside a heavy cloak of reality
        Finally, it gets cold
            after sunset

FROM ASPEN TO DENVER

I drove today
through the magic mountains.
My eyes, feasting
on an imposing landscape
spreading like
a multilayer painting
with ever changing images:
spruces and pines hanging
on the verticality
of stratified, crimsom rocks.
Snow, trees, sky and clouds
embraced in a sacred communion
with the Mighty Cosmos.
Skiers descending
like ants on a milky slope.

Today, I entered
the Cathedral of Nature.

MOLECULAR JOURNEY

At the time when
my telluric privilege
to consume oxygen
or making decisions
has come to an end,
I would like to convey
to my beloved children,
my siblings and good friends
that I prefer
the fleeting, terminal flame
which shall spread
my molecules to the wind
rather than the asphyxiant
weight of a tombstone
which shall hide
for centuries
the infinite pleasure
of being a tree,
a flower or cloud,
part of other space,
part of other time.

SCAR OF INNOCENCE

*(Reading the book "The kite runner"
I ran into a child with cleft lip who
brought to my memory many other children
I operated on in the past with this similar affliction)*

*Don't fret, little angel.
Maybe God was tired,
careless or simply,
He didn't care about
your unfinished anatomy
or perhaps it is all
a genetic mis-step.*

*It has been said:
"It is better to be hurt
by an ugly truth
than comforted
by a beautiful lie."*

*Please trust my hands,
little angel
and when it's time
for you to talk
you shall have
your own sound,
when it's time
to be happy
you shall have
your own smile.*

INQUIRING

Did you ever wonder
what the wind feels
when, tenaciously, it embraces
the tree tops?.
Or the ocean waves feel
when they kiss
the moist lips
of a sandy beach?.
Or perhaps,
what the rain feels
when it washes
the dry face
of the parched land?
Or the moon feels
when its silvery tongue
licks the roof tops
of the slumbering city?
Or maybe, what Earth feels
when man squanders its bounties
giving back so little?

WHEN TOMORROW COMES

*Please, be patient
when tomorrow comes,
when the symphony of my awareness
is no longer tuned
to my surroundings.*

*Please, learn to forgive me
if I repeat myself,
if I forget a name
or some meaningful date,
maybe your birthday
or perhaps mine.*

*When you see me
technologically inept,
be patient explaining the secrets
of the internet.*

*Don't feel sad
angry or ashamed,
if I don't wear
the outfit of your taste*

*Please, be patient
when my steps
are not as brisk as yours,
when to cross the street
I need your hand.
Remember…
when you were a toddler
you needed mine.*

      C.
        P.

WHEN TOMORROW COMES

Please, be patient
when tomorrow comes,
when the raspberry of my awareness
is no longer toned
to my surroundings.

Please, listen to & place me
if I repeat myself,
if I forget a name
or some meaningful date,
maybe your birthday
or perhaps mine.

When you see me
technologically inept,
be patient explaining the source
of the internet.

Don't feel sad,
angry or unhappy,
if I don't relish
the surprise of your visit.

Please, be patient
when my steps
are not as brisk as yours,
when it may take time
to find your hand.
Remember,
what you are is a reality
you needed anoint.

C. T.